Sons and Others

Published by 404 Ink Limited
www.404Ink.com
@404Ink

Please note: Some references include URLs which may change or be unavailable
after publication of this book. All references within endnotes were accessible
and accurate as of August 2022 but may experience link rot from there on in.

Editing: Laura Jones & Heather McDaid
Proofreading: Heather McDaid
Typesetting: Laura Jones
Cover design: Luke Bird
Co-founders and publishers of 404 Ink:
Heather McDaid & Laura Jones

Print ISBN: 978-1-912489-64-0
Ebook ISBN: 978-1-912489-65-7

Printed and bound in Great Britain by Clays Ltd, Elcograf S.p.A.

Sons and Others

On Loving Male Survivors

Tanaka Mhishi

Inklings

Contents

Contents

Content Note

Please note that there are depictions and descriptions of both adult and child sexual assault and rape throughout *Sons and Others*.

Introduction
Asking better questions

'Hands up who has seen the Jim Carrey movie *The Mask*?'

Of the eighty people in the audience, maybe forty-five raise their hands. I let the question linger, look around the auditorium. The faces are inquisitive, some bordering on the suspicious.

'Keep your hand up,' I say, 'if you remember the rape scene in it.'

A cascade of hands fall and confusion ripples through the room. I nod. As expected.

This is how I sometimes begin talks on male survivors of sexual violence. The scene in question happens near the denouement of the film, where the protagonist stops en route to rescuing the female lead to sexually assault two mechanics who wronged him earlier in the story. It's played for laughs, the camera cutting away to a lightbulb while comic book *boings* and *thwacks* are laid over the mechanics screaming. It's a throwaway gag that tells us a lot about our culture's attitude to male survivors. As the evening's event unfolds I unpick the myths that it reinforces; that sexual violence against men is funny, bizarre, outlandish. The talk segues into my own experiences, into the broader contexts and forces at play in the lives of men who experience sexual violence.

Afterwards, a woman comes up to me.

'I couldn't believe that,' she said, 'I showed that film to my *kids*.'

I nod. It is, after all, a kid's movie.

*

Most of us grew up in this world, one which treated sexual violence against men as a harmless joke. I also watched *The Mask* as a child and barely noticed the scene. It was only in my twenties, as I began navigating life as a male rape survivor, that I began to notice the casual derision directed at men like me which is threaded through our culture. How could it be otherwise, when we have spent years being cued to laugh at this phenomenon, that we struggle to take it seriously?

The history of our conversations on sexual violence has, for understandable reasons, focused on women's voices and experiences. The data indicates that women are still the majority of victims,[1] and most of our communities and public services are not doing enough to prevent this violence. Most of the perpetrators of violence against women are men and it's easy to fall into the position that male survivors' stories are exceptions or irrelevances. The fact is, though, that we share a world and our experiences are closely interwoven.

In the UK around one in six men will experience some form of sexual violence.[2] Recent data suggests that twice that number will experience sexual harassment in the workplace. Among gay and bisexual men, the rate of sexual violence is higher, hovering at around 47%.[3] That's around two men per football team who will be assaulted or abused, five boys in a mixed class of thirty who will go on to be sexually harassed at work, and half the men in a gay club. The average British woman probably dates one or two male survivors in her lifetime, and there's a decent chance that she will marry or mother one. Male survivors also far outnumber male perpetrators of sexual abuse in the general population,[4] but we have historically been prone to denial about our experiences. One study found that men have been been less likely to recognise their own ordeals as sexual abuse; as many as 84% percent of men who had had experiences which met the legal definition of sexual abuse did not describe themselves as victims or survivors.[5] We don't know how this has changed over the past few years.

If we widen this thought out to any include unwanted sexual experience (including harassment, groping or sexual activity with an adult before the age of consent) some recent data suggests that as many as half of men will be affected.[6] We do not know how this fits into the broader picture of sexual harassment in public and private spaces and how often the perpetrators are the same people who are perpetrating violence against women and girls.

'What happened to you?'

This is the first question that people ask me as a male rape survivor. They often don't want to talk about it at all, and the conversation is turned, firmly but gracefully, towards something less contentious. Anything will do. Religious taboo, major political upheaval, cryptocurrency. People would rather talk about anything else. But one on one, when the lights are low, people ask, 'What happened to you?'

It's a trap. Like most of the questions survivors are asked, the question dictates the terms of its answer. My rape, and the assaults which preceded it, are some of the least interesting things about me. The world is lousy with survivors; you probably pass ten of us on the way to work.

Knowing that someone is a survivor tells you nothing about them. It does not tell you that they make fantastic pasta sauce or spent a summer working in a ranch restaurant in Wyoming, or once patented a new kind of orthopedic shoe. It does not tell you that they are a good father or a great daughter, a ukulele player, or a great writer.

The second and third questions are equally useless.

'How can that happen to a man?'

'Why didn't you fight back?'

We see representations of sexual violence against women frequently in our society, from the infamous scenes in *Game of Thrones* to the *Carry On* movies. These scenes are fraught and damaging in many ways, but they are at least a clear mythology to push back on. By contrast, sexual violence against men has historically been framed as as 'bizarre' or exceptional.

Of course, we all have questions. But I think we are asking the wrong ones.

A week after I was raped in 2015, I took myself down to the Jubilee Library in Brighton, where I was a student, in search of answers to my questions – to the questions that many male survivors ask in the wake of being raped or sexually assaulted.

I wanted to know what would happen next. Would I ever want to have sex again? Would I be able to fall in love – and would anyone want to fall in love with me? If so, who? Would people want to hire me if they knew I was a rape survivor? Would I now be a horrible father? Should I tell my family, and, if so, how?

These are altogether more practical questions, questions that, as the 1 in 6 figure indicates, millions of men are grappling with. In the UK, that translates to upwards of five million men who are attempting to find their own answers to these questions.

You, reading this, are sure to know some of us. But the silence around the sexual abuse of men means that he is unlikely to tell you. Even if you are his parent or his partner. Even if you are raising children together or working side by side. Even if he is your father. Even if you, whatever your gender, are a survivor or victim of abuse yourself.

If we want to know each other better, and if we want to love – and be loved by – men who have experienced abuse then our thinking has to change. We need to stop seeing male survivors as a slice of the pie chart, an exception, or an oddity. Instead, we need to grapple with what this experience means for all of us and our relationships in a world that is struggling to move towards equality and liberation. We need to meet male survivors on their own terms.

And we need to ask better questions.

Some of the questions in this book have no easy answers, because there is a lot we don't know. Currently, most research on sexual violence is centred on female survivors of male perpetrated violence. There are sporadic pieces of research on male survivors' experiences, and a smattering of studies which deal with the experiences of non-binary people. Proponents of this approach, which most people call 'gender specific', point out that there is no sense in pretending that men and women are having the same experiences of sexual violence, harassment and harm. There are others who argue for a 'gender neutral' way of understanding these crimes, who tend to believe that while the impact may be unevenly distributed, the feelings evoked by sexual violence are largely the same, and that it's not right for some groups to be supported while others are not.

To my mind, both approaches are incomplete. Both have their merits, but they also mean that we are missing the rich and diverse landscapes in which survivors live their actual lives.

When I was raped, it was a female friend who showed up to my side in the months after. She made sure I was eating and taking the medication that would prevent me from contracting HIV. After a disastrous police interview a month later, I had to call her from the side of a main road. I had been trying to calculate where the trucks would be going their fastest so that I could throw myself under one. She cleared her evening to take care of me. Years later, after she was raped, I was with her in the moment she admitted to herself what had happened, and she half-cried, half-laughed, doubling over in shock.

Her trauma and my trauma are different beasts, shaped by our different experiences of gender, sexuality and race. They happened for different reasons. But we were parts of each other's journeys towards recovery. Our experiences happened alongside each other, and ours are intertwined in a way that neither a gender neutral nor gender specific way of thinking can capture.

Over the past seven years I have worked with people of all genders who have widely different experiences of sexual violence, and I can tell you that there is more hope in this work than you would possibly believe. For every gut-twisting story of abuse I have encountered, I have also been blown away by the wisdom, compassion and courage in those who work with trauma; both their own and others. To capture and share this wisdom we need neither neutrality nor specificity, but diversity.

One of the great gifts I received early in my career was from a colleague who described our jobs as patchwork. A single square of fabric, no matter how diligently made, will not do much against the cold. We need to join it up to those around it to create adequate protection. This book is about that work of joining up, stitching together, linking hands. It is about holding the male survivor experience alongside others and thinking about how we fit into our society together.

One in six men. Probably more. I hope that as you are reading this you will think about the men in your life.

About your father, your uncles, your brothers. About the men on your favourite football team or, if you are someone who is attracted to men, the people you have fancied, kissed, loved, had sex with. If you are a male survivor who is reading this I hope you will also think about the other people in your life, men, women and non-binary people, who may have similar experiences to you.

This is not just about supporting men and boys who have experienced sexual violence. It is about a web of connected experiences and solidarities – often messy, sometimes uncomfortable, but always real and worthwhile.

Chapter 1
Sons

A traumatic memory does not work like any other kind of memory. When I call them up, the process is graceless and spasmodic, as though I am wrenching diseased tissue away from my spine. You never know how deep the rot goes, it's been part of you that long.

Here is what I remember.

I am in a hotel pool, kidney shaped, on the southwest coast of Sri Lanka. Our family have been coming here for years, watching it cycle through phases of dilapidation and regeneration as though they were seasons. I am maybe eight years old.

I'm not sure where my parents are, but as an only child I'm used to playing by myself. I have an expansive imaginative life, full of adventures and characters plucked from books. I can pretend to be a merman in the pool; I'm a good swimmer and I enjoy opening my eyes underwater and seeing the sunlight stretch its gentle columns through the pool.

As I surface, a spray of water hits me in the face. I look over, and a man is there. He is local – I don't expect him to speak English and my Sinhalese is weak. But he has a playful look on his face so I splash him back.

He dodges. Smiles. Splashes me. I retaliate, mimicking his cupped hand so that the volume of water is greater. He answers with another volley, and I dodge to my right. He is silhouetted, so I can't quite see him, just that he is dark skinned with a moustache and a neat haircut.

We go back and forth, and I'm pleased to realise that I am dodging his sprays of water more than he is dodging mine. I'm winning; he is over-favouring one hand. All I have to do is be prepared to dive further to my right.

We go back and forth for maybe three or four minutes. He advances on me, and I laugh in delight. This is what I've been waiting for. I flip onto my back and kick my legs, creating a shower of water that erupts over him at just the right moment. I see the sky, the blue water, the green of the plants, taste the chlorine and the triumph of outsmarting a grown up.

And that is the moment when I notice the open gate, which leads out to the beach. At the same time, I realise that I have been manoeuvred round so that he is between me and the hotel, and that the gate must be open because he came through it. That the splashing was calculated to push me away from wherever my parents might be.

I am in trouble. I am in big, big trouble.

A split second later, I feel a hand against my ankle. I turn around in the water and inhale, cough, drag myself upright. Another hand just barely grazes my calf. Then, with all the speed of a child with a gold swimming certificate and a healthy dose of adrenaline, I swim up to the nearest group of people, a family of German-speaking tourists who are round the corner. The three or four seconds it takes me to reach them are some of the most frightening of my life, but I make it, gasping and shivering.

Instinctively, I do not tell them what was happening, or look round to see if the man has followed me. When my mother comes to collect me from the pool, I do not tell her either.

In fact, I won't tell anyone about this incident for nearly twenty years.

The abuse of any child is profoundly disturbing – not just for the victim, but for their family, and feelings of shame, guilt and blame are all but inevitable. Most often, this blame falls onto mothers, even though they are rarely the perpetrators of abuse. This idea that mothers hold the exclusive responsibility for safeguarding their children is a manifestation of sexist or traditional values. But where the abused child is a boy, it often goes further.

The abuse of boys challenges the traditional conception of gender, and in response family systems often cleave closer to regressive ideas. The idea that their sons might venture outside traditional masculinity – by being gay, by being sexually submissive, or even by exhibiting traditionally 'feminine' traits like empathy, collaboration and tenderness – becomes tied to the experience of abuse itself, and so parents often default to modelling patriarchal values as a response. As one researcher writes: 'While theories that blame mothers often focus on intrafamilial CSA [Child Sex Abuse], a number of them view mothers as liable for the abuse because maternal employment is seen as a hindrance to a woman's ability to safe-guard her child from the abuser.'[1]

Many mothers will decrease or even end their participation in the workforce following the revelation of sexual abuse of their sons.

It's important to remember that while mothers are often unfairly blamed for not noticing abuse, this blame is as likely to come from within themselves as it is from broader family systems. The fear and shame that mothers of sexually abused boys feel is a contributing factor in everyone's silence.

I kept silent about my near miss at the hotel pool instinctively because I knew my mother would blame herself. I was aware, even as a child, that she faced significant scrutiny as a disabled mother, that there had been questions about her fitness and that it was important for me to present myself as a happy, polite and intelligent child. It sounds shockingly grown up for an eight year old to grasp, but I sensed that keeping silent about the incident was the safest thing for our family. If I told her – or anyone – then other people would start watching her more closely, berating her, blaming her. She would be less likely to allow me to go on adventures in pools, or with friends and relatives. As a boy, I felt pressured to protect her, as a child I wanted to stay free, and as a son I did not want her to be criticised or blamed.

I was lucky to avoid the abuse which I sensed approaching, but even if I hadn't, it's easy to understand why I might have kept silent about it. In a system which ascribes most of the blame to mothers for not safe-guarding their sons.

What kind of system could we have instead? For a start, we know that families who take a more fluid, adaptive approach to gendered roles tend to be more successful in supporting boys who have been abused to overcome their trauma.[2] A focus on understanding abused boys, rather than 'fixing' them helps rebuild a sense of safety and autonomy. Beyond that, the overwhelming burden of ensuring children's safety needs to be moved beyond parents and guardians, and into the community. This can feel like a risk, especially since most abuse happens in community contexts. But counter-intuitive as it seems, the most effective response to abuse is not to withdraw trust in the outside world, but to repair it. This isn't work for parents themselves to do, it's about the broader community stepping up to support families in keeping their children safe. It's the German family, whose presence and willingness to let me stay with them made it impossible for the man in the pool to keep up his attempts at abuse. We're doing some of that work already, it's the basis of much of our safeguarding policies but it also means funding services for male survivors of childhood sexual abuse. It means therapeutic support for mums of abused children, and abused boys specifically. It means other family members taking on regular, active, safe childcaring. All too often, that's not happening.

Fathers, meanwhile, tended to withdraw from caring activities, like participating in family therapy or having conversations about their sons' wellbeing where those activities that might lead to them engaging with the subject of their son's abuse. In fact, when boys wanted to talk about these issues, many dads abscond from parenting activities altogether.[3]

Those activities which remain are often centred around reinforcing their sons masculinity and gender conformity. One scholar notes that 'to "fix" what had happened, many fathers' gendered strategic plans stressed the need to do more masculine activities with their sons. This included signing their sons up for sports teams, roughhousing, and consciously rewarding hetero-sexuality. These fathers hoped that these formulaic masculine activities would hinder their sons from becoming gay and (re)construct a masculine, hetero-sexual identity. The gender strategies of most men included condemning any same-sex affection and the blatant objectification of girls and women.'[4]

This last point is one of the hardest instincts to under-stand; the idea that fathers might enact neglect, homo-phobia and misogyny as a (misguided) form of care for their sons. On an objective level it is easy to see that not only does pushing their sons into these behaviours not only puts them at risk of further violence – boys who learn that asking for help will result in their being shut down are not likely to speak up again – it also builds habits which will inhibit their ability to exist in gender-diverse survivor spaces as adults.

But if we understand that these behaviours are moti-vated largely by fathers' genuine desire to do what is best for their children then the way in which we challenge this behaviour becomes vitally important. For a parent who is devastated, angry and frightened about their child's future, it's easy to default to the traditional gendered behaviour which feels safe.

The fact that mothers are more likely than fathers to be survivors also means that additional support might be needed. When I was raped many of the mother figures in my life were not only shocked but disturbed by their own resurgent experiences of abuse. One even confessed that my rape made her question the way she was raising her son. 'As a feminist I feel like there's this huge pressure to make sure he grows up as good man. I sort of feel like I've under-worried about him being a victim in the way I was.'

The fact is that this woman – accomplished, compassionate and intelligent – almost never stopped worrying about the people around her, often at the expense of her own wellbeing. But as willing as she was to add this worry to her list, it doesn't seem fair. Fathers too need to be part of the psychological labour that goes into their sons' healing. The research suggests that explicit equality within the home; sharing cooking, cleaning and nurturing responsibilities and splitting absence from work can be a valuable strategy for families supporting abused boys. Men's role in explicitly rejecting mother-blaming is also a powerful tool, even or especially where that blame comes from other women or the mother herself. Here again, the role of community as an enabler is important.

*

It's difficult to understand the episode in the pool without thinking about race. Sri Lankan culture, like many in South Asia, values lighter skin tones than darker ones. Thrice subjugated by European empires, Sri Lanka's capital Colombo is still pockmarked with old colonial hotels. My Sri Lankan grandparents took afternoon tea, my grandmother grew up in a house where the butler wore full white tie in the sweltering heat. In our family the Christmas cakes are Dutch, our stair railings Portuguese, our language English. Most of my mother's friends did the right thing for well-brought up Sri Lankan girls; that is, they went to university, got respectable jobs in law, medicine or accounting, married well-brought up Sri Lankan boys, had babies and ran households.

They did not do what my mother did, which was to run away to university, take up with a Black African Catholic priest, become an artist and sell her paintings from the railings by Russell Square in London.

As a mixed-race child with no white parent, I was born, nine years later, into the highest risk racial demographic for experiencing sexual violence, although none of us knew it then. While non-white mixed people face the highest risk, we know that mixed children in general are more at risk of sexual violence than people whose parents are the same race.[5] Mixed race men are twice as likely as white men to report being sexually assaulted.[6]

We don't know why.

It may be that sex offenders are more likely to notice children who are visually different to those around them. Or they might gamble on those children being more culturally isolated than other children, less securely attached and thus less likely to speak up. As alone at the poolside and a little easier to pick off.

For me, part of why I didn't speak up about that day at the pool was that my presence in Sri Lankan society was so contingent. My clearly African heritage, my British accent, the fact that I didn't speak any Sinhalese, all of these meant that I had to compromise. I had to be compliant, intelligent, quiet and capable. I had to not draw attention to myself except as a precocious intellect. These factors got me into the habit of silence around discomfort.

The beach where I was nearly abducted was notorious for hosting 'beach boys', young men and boys who were victims of systematic sexual abuse, largely at the hands of Western foreigners. One of my aunts, who ran a charity supporting children on the beaches, remarked that parents often depended on the income from sexually exploiting their sons to supplement the poverty wages they drew in from fishing and domestic labour. The boys were told that it was their duty to support their families, tapping into their nascent male identities as providers. She described boys as young as eight – as young as me at the time – emerging from the large, foreigner owned holiday homes clutching fistfuls of rupees in their hands. The only potential protection for these boys was, and remains, Sri Lanka's vague anti-homosexuality laws. The age of consent in Sri Lanka is sixteen in most circumstances, but the penal code restricts legal consequences to male perpetrators of abuse against girls.[7] Agencies on the ground note that 'as is common in many other conflict-affected countries, Sri Lankan law does not recognise and therefore does not proscribe male rape.'[8]

The waves of abuse came and went with the tides themselves; most of the local children had fishermen as fathers. When the catch was bad, they would be sent out to 'work', their 'wages' often going towards their education (school in Sri Lanka is free, but children often have to pay for the books, materials and even furniture within the schoolroom as a condition of enrolment). In this system the abuse of the beach boys is deeply, systemically entrenched in the local economy. The wealthy men who came to exploit these Sri Lankan boys were mostly white and mostly from the West and, in a continuation of the colonial project, had built a system where social mobility for local people was dependent on the sexual exploitation of brown bodies.

In some areas of the Global South we see a parallel dynamic enacted by women, typically wealthy white women who desire racialised sexual contact with Black men, who have led to a thriving trade in male sex workers in places like West Africa and the Caribbean.[9] These women typically choose men who are structurally disadvantaged relative to them on a number of other characteristics; age, race, education and income. It is likely that most of these men, unlike the boys in Sri Lanka and elsewhere in South Asia, are adults, and it's important not to conflate childhood sexual exploitation with adult sex workers. But the fact that these white women, many of whom are the descendants of slavers, are gravitating towards buying sex from men of communities devastated by the transatlantic slave trade reveals something deeply uncomfortable about these interactions. There is, after all, no shortage of male sex workers closer to home, which suggests that these women are deliberately seeking relationships in which they have power over a man.

Growing up, I was deeply aware of the gaze of white girls and women on my body. My school – technically a state school, but one which boasted a clutch of children whose parents were Members of Parliament, its own lake, and a multi-million pound income from a centuries old trust – was where I first encountered this discomfort.

I took two buses every morning. On a good day the journey was somewhere around an hour, on a bad one closer to eighty minutes. If you missed the school bus, the nearest alternative route involved a nearly half hour walk from the closest town up to the site, meaning there was no such thing as being 'slightly late'. But it was a good school, with good results, and so every day I made the journey out of London, past the huge houses and the fields and across the M25. Usually I went in and out with friends who lived nearby. But on the rare occasions I was on my own I knew to avoid a certain group of girls in the year above me.

It started slowly. The asked me if I was gay, tried to trick me into a limp wristed posture to take a picture. Then they began sliding pencils into my hair from behind, until I made sure it was cut off. This, generally, was my approach to their antics. I didn't even really count it as bullying; I was a teenager and decidedly superior. Besides, they certainly weren't as scary as their male counterparts.

As I approached fourteen though, the timbre of their harassment switched. The bus peeled away down a country road and one of them said, 'How big do you think Tanaka's dick is?' I remember my stomach lurching, being very careful not to let my discomfort show. Being very careful not to let them know that they'd got to me.

They continued a discussion about the size, shape and colour of my genitals while we drove out of Hertfordshire and didn't change the subject until we crossed the M25. They knew I was there, they kept sneaking glances at me. For the next few weeks, they would corner me in the corridor, asking for confirmation. I don't quite remember how I responded, but I do remember how it made me feel; sick and confused but also slightly mad, as though

I were blowing the whole thing out of proportion. They were only asking, after all.

There were only two other Black boys in my year, neither of whom I was close to. And it wasn't until I was older that I realised that this might count as sexual harassment, or that it was deeply racialised. Their male counterparts had similar conversations; I once spent nearly forty minutes listening to a group of my peers laugh about how disgusting my body was while I sat on the bus behind them. I was also aware of much more dangerous forms of sexual victimisation against my friends who were girls, one of whom was in such an abusive relationship that her boyfriend attacked any boy she so much as stood next to.

The next leg of my bus journey, through a slightly rough part of London, involved dealing with the police officers who patrolled the bus station. Again, when I was with my white friends I was left alone. But if they spotted me coming out of the newsagents alone, or simply running to catch the bus their hackles could go up. There was one particular officer who always missed shaving the wisps of hair around his Adam's apple and absolutely had it in for me. He once threatened to arrest me under the anti-terrorism legislation because I was making suspicious images of the station. I was sketching it.

So much of my transition from boyhood to manhood felt like the withdrawal of protection. As a Black man in particular, my teenage years were spent in a mind-bending hinterland, where the world viewed me both as a vulnerable child and as a dangerous threat. Neither of those perceptions enabled me to stand up for myself, or for my female friends who were experiencing violence. The response offered to me when I was subjected to racialised harassment or sexualised harm was contradictory.

Ignore it but fight back.

Don't be aggressive but don't be a doormat.

Don't make a big deal.

We have come a long way since then in understanding that boys have a role to play in disrupting and preventing violence against women and girls, and there are any number of educational programmes and interventions which seek to engage young men in these conversations. I've delivered and even helped design some of these myself. But what many of them lack is the will to engage with the substantial portion of young men who will be victims of violence of many kinds; racial, sexual and economic, and who are offered a vision of manhood which does not involve the right to safety and protection. These interventions often come about because of an urgent need to address sexual harassment against women and girls. In a classroom setting where time is short, the instinct is to have a laser-like emphasis on confronting misogyny. The importance of this goes without saying, but I believe we are missing crucial groundwork, and that groundwork includes engaging with the inevitable presence of boy survivors and victims who are in the room.

During the few years where I worked with young people on consent education I came across three fundamental beliefs about equality and safety that went unchallenged in school environments.

1. Boys and girls have equal capacities, rights and should be treated equally.
2. Violence against women and girls is wrong.
3. Experiencing and using violence is a normal and unremarkable part of being a man.

It is impossible to hold all three of these beliefs wholeheartedly. Many of the boys who were resistant to feminist interventions which emphasised the first two beliefs found these discussions difficult precisely because they had been taught to minimise their own experiences of violence in line with the third belief. When others made them uncomfortable, including in ways which involved actions which would be defined as sexual harassment (showing them porn, sexualised comments, non-consensual image taking and sharing), their response was much like mine; put up with it and shut up about it, laugh it off, pretend to enjoy it. These young men did not see why girls shouldn't have to do the same. When we answered that these behaviours are wrong in any context, against any young person, they often went quiet and thoughtful.

However, during one workshop with a group of young men who knew each other, one of them spoke up. 'This is ridiculous.' He pointed at the whiteboard on which I and my co-facilitator had detailed a list of behaviours that constituted sexual harassment. 'You can't say all these things are abuse, or that I've been abused.'

The silence that came afterwards was one which I'm afraid to say I fumbled as a facilitator. I didn't know what to say. My co-facilitator did as we were trained to do, which was to refocus on the disproportionate impact on women and girls in their community. The session went on. I sat there. And as we approached lunchtime, I was unable to shake the feeling that we had failed. It was not that discussing and acknowledging that disproportionate impact was wrong, but there was something utterly dismissive about the haste with which we moved from an actual male survivor in order to talk about the theory of how they could be better men in the future. We did not manage to hold space for the existential questions that we had brought up for this young man.

The fact is that in any group of boys who we are engaging in a discussion of feminism and the prevention of violence against women, there will be a cohort of survivors. Some of whom will only begin to grapple with their experiences through being invited to consider the harm that male violence against women does in the wider world. They will only have the realisation that they have been failed, exploited or unprotected in the very moment that they are called to prevent failure, exploitation and a lack of safety. They will realise they are victims in the same moment they understand that the world sees them as potential perpetrators.

That's a lot to expect a child to take on at once.

We need to shift the order of things. It's absolutely right for boys to be raised to challenge misogyny, and the parts of our culture which enable rape and abuse of women. More than right, it's frankly our only hope. But we cannot layer a message of equality and anti-violence on top of one which sees violence against men and boys as unimportant and expect it to stick. It simply won't, not unless we have unpicked the idea that the safeguarding of boys is the exclusive responsibility of mothers and their sons and we have addressed the ways in which boy survivors are failed by broader society.

What would a world of supported parents of sexually abused boys look like?

For a start, a radically engaged form of fatherhood; one which is backed by policies and communities. Equal paid parental leave for parents of all abused children is probably part of the picture there. For boys, a programme of healing that involves a wide variety of activities, not just therapy, not just stereotypically masculine pursuits. Sexual violence services for women will need additional resources to support mothers who have their own sexual trauma and find themselves parenting abused boys. Services for men will have to expand their remit to supporting all parents of male survivors. LGBT+ services will have to deal with their clients as *parents* as well as survivors. And all three will have to dedicate time to collaborating, building an infrastructure that does not just focus on supporting individual survivors, but on communities of care, safety and healing.

If we can do this, if we can put time, money and effort into the idea that boys deserve to be protected from all forms of violence, I believe we will be able to raise a generation of men committed to anti-violence, anti-sexist practice, and genuine safety for all of us. We cannot afford the alternative.

Chapter 2
Friends

M is my oldest friend and we call each other the Opposite Twins. Opposites because of how different we are on paper and twins because of how alike we are inside. Her parents were a deeply cool lesbian couple whose house always smelled of butter, strawberries and clean wood. They were a theatre director and a teacher and would have loved her to do something in the arts. Mine gently pushed me towards maths and sciences; coached me through entrance exams for tough schools and encouraged me to do a practical degree. M has a particle physics PhD and I write books about sexual violence for a living. We even look like opposites; she's the kind of ginger who is in danger of sunburn from a particularly bright lightbulb.

But we call ourselves twins because we are also deeply similar. We both discovered we were bisexual around the same time, both love to bake. We've kissed a good portion of the same people, love the same kinds of music. Sometimes we even finish each other's sentences. When M got married a few years ago I flew out to her in-laws in Virginia. We made the wedding cake together in their kitchen, using her red velvet recipe for the body of it and smothering it with my vegan buttercream in swirls of purple, pink and cream. It's one of those deep, good relationships that can be picked up easily even if we haven't spoken for a few years.

M was in London when I first began talking publicly about being raped. She came with me to a festival where I was on a panel with other male survivors. I remember little of the talk itself, but I do remember feeling her stand next to me as we walked up the road towards the venue; the warmth coming off her.

More than any other experience in my life, the rape changed the topography of my friendships. If I imagine a spectrum of helpful to unhelpful reactions, the women in my life clustered at the two extremes. Most of them opened their hearts to me with shocking levels of empathy and support. It was the women in my life who made sure I was eating properly and that I was taking my medication, kept me safe when I was suicidal, hugged me, walked with me, advocated for me and generally went above and beyond to take care of me in ways which really should have been the job of everyone in my life. I doubt I would be alive if not for them. There were also a smaller number who reacted to me with an equally shocking level of contempt. Two female friends cut me out of their lives immediately; one of them later laughed about my rape and described it as 'friendly fire' at a house party when she thought I was in the other room. Some others withdrew from me slowly. Later, one of them – a bright woman who I'd known and looked up to at university – got in touch to apologise for dropping me. She said, more or less, that she'd spent so much time worrying about her female friends' safety that it felt almost unfair for her to have to worry about mine too. Part of having male friends, for her, was feeling comfortable that they were safe. On some level she seemed to feel almost cheated.

And my male friends? I didn't have many at that time; my English Literature course was, typically, pretty sparse in the men department. But I did have one. I knew somehow that if I didn't tell people what had happened quickly I never would.

The buildings around where Elliot lived were brilliant white and butter yellow where they faced the public street. Ducking down into his side alley the walls were suddenly dripping with mould, the paving stones a little more uneven. The courtyard in front of Elliot's house was dominated by the neighbours' car; a four-wheel drive monster which looked like it had been through at least six apocalypses. I had to squeeze past it to get to the door.

He was drunk when he answered, but not excessively so. I ducked into a low, warm hall, following him, a beer swaying in his hand as he led me back to the living room.

I told my friends I'd hurt my leg as an explanation for my absence at university, but in front of his fireplace, while he sat in the peeling Chesterfield, I mumbled the truth, placing it into the low ceilinged room like a bomb.

The corners of Elliot's mouth began to twitch. He giggled, covering his mouth. Then he laughed, he properly laughed, he actually slapped his thigh. I was bewildered. Had he misheard? What else does 'I was raped' sound like?

'Fuck me, that's rough man,' he said. 'You know what you should do?'

I sighed internally. *Go to the police*, I thought, *that's what he's about to say*. I had little enough energy to tell him I'd already done that and been told off for being 'too sensitive'.

'You should go out and just bang some drunk girl, like brutal you know? Get it out of your system.'

If there had been a fire in the grate it would have blown out, that's how hard I sucked in my breath. Where the hell did that come from? Everything I'd read about sexual violence had led me to expect that I'd be chastised for dressing or acting wrong, not told to go out and commit my own assault to even the score. And what was with the laughing? What was going on?

I know now that Elliot's suggestion was a classic example of the gender affirmation tactic writ large. Here's the logic underneath it: first off, being raped is something which happens to women. Second, being feminised, not being violated, is the most degrading thing which can happen to a man. Third, the obvious cure is to engage in behaviours which reaffirm masculinity. In Elliot's head committing an act of rape against an intoxicated woman was one of them.

Elliot was proving what research has indicated to be true, that the victim blaming of male survivors is the dancing partner of similar behaviours deployed against women.[1] Men lead, women follow, and the rape of men is traumatic, tense, humorous, because it disrupts this established order. In other words, our society doesn't struggle to talk about male survivors because it's too painful. We struggle because it's too weird. While women who are raped by men are a manifestation of how gender stereotypes can devastate an individual's lives, male survivors are walking, talking, living ruptures in the patriarchal narrative. And that makes people nervous.

Gender affirmation strategies, like Elliot's suggestion, are ways to deal with this weirdness, this rupture. They are attempts to save maleness at the expense of a real man or boy who is suffering and they can be breath-taking in their short-sightedness.

I should say at this point that Elliot was, probably, joking. I suspect he'd be mortified to know that his comment landed like a lead balloon on our friendship. But it made me deeply frightened of him. Nothing in our friendship thus far had indicated to me that he found sexual violence funny or acceptable. In fact it had never come up.

My body reacted to him like he was dangerous. My heart was running fast in my chest in a rhythm that screamed *get out, get out, get out*. At the same time, I struggled to give him the benefit of the doubt. He was just trying to help. Or was he? I didn't know, and between us we didn't have the language to figure it out.

When you are raped and you talk about it, most of the time, you have to do so to suit someone else's language. Whether that person is a police officer or a journalist or a counsellor or your mother, you have to put what has happened in their terms. And for men, the terms are narrower, the vocabulary more vague, the suspension of disbelief tauter and begging to be snapped.

The rape of men is a new concept. Before the law changed to recognise male survivors in 1994 what happened to me wouldn't have counted as 'rape', not legally. And if my attacker had had a vagina, it wouldn't have counted either. At the time of writing, in the UK you cannot legally be raped by someone without a penis. There is sentencing parity; the law in theory recognises that either experience can be equally devastating. But the word isn't used. There are some jurisdictions where men cannot be raped in the eyes of the law, or even where 'rape' is no longer used in any criminal justice context, but doctors still record rape and use 'rape kits' in treatment, so that in the short journey from hospital to courthouse the word is both bestowed and withdrawn.

Words are important, that much I knew. And I was learning that a lack of words can be even more important.

There is a depth charge which happens when you tell another person you have been raped. People are careful around you in certain ways. It seems unequivocal, they know what has happened. Saying you were sexually assaulted is easier on those who have to hear it. It gives them room to ask what happened, even if they don't do it out loud. It does not force people to imagine a particular act, and it does not make the body untouchable in the same way.

I remember leaving the basement flat by the station, looking up at a yellowish grey sky and feeling that word, 'rape', bloom in my mind. I remember how heavy it was in my head, so heavy I became dizzy and had to grab onto a wrought iron fence to my right. I remember watching the water through a grate and the grain of the tarmac. I remember the word 'RAPE' emblazoned in my head as I practically crawled past a boutique with a chaise longue and a Lolita dress in the window.

I remember calling my nearest friend and saying exactly these words: 'I think I've just been raped.'

I wanted to laugh, almost. Like death, when it's new, and so impossible that you still think the world is playing a trick on you.

And sometimes, when I've told people I was raped, they have acted as though I've pulled a trick on them. The receptionist who admitted me to A&E didn't just roll her eyes, she rolled her entire neck. My ex, who had driven me to the hospital, had given the information bluntly. 'He's just been raped.' I saw clearly her eyebrows go up into her fringe, her eyeballs swivel. I remember thinking, *Oh god, I absolutely cannot do this* and realising that you cannot just *say* that, and, *Who cares if I get HIV or if I'm bleeding inside, I need to be away from this hospital right now.*

My ex wouldn't have let me leave though. She took me by the arm into the waiting room. I sat there, feeling something wet in my jeans that I didn't dare think about, trying to figure out how to put what had happened into words for the doctor. I knew I had to say this the right way if I wanted to be taken seriously. The eyeroll kept playing on a loop in my head.

You can tell when you've 'said it wrong' by the way people withdraw from you, the folding of arms. I learned to tell the story of my rape to suit the listener. As I waded through the many bureaucracies of rape – this clinic and that, this officer or the other, this form for the university and so on – I gathered a kind of poker hand of ways to share this story. Sometimes I slid the fact of my rape into conversation and insisted it not be a big deal. For the more gory-minded I let the story sit there, unrolled, in its Hitchcockian horror, half enjoying the discomfort I cause simply by existing, before summing it up.

This is one way:

On the evening of February 9th, 2014, I arranged to meet a man in a bar on St James Street in Brighton at around 8.30pm. We met and socialised there for a few hours with his friend, after which we went back to a house near the station and had some consensual sexual contact. When I refused to have anal sex without a condom he pushed, persuaded, relented and then, when I was half asleep, raped me.

This is another:

It was the February of a winter that lingered like a bad guest. My singleness was just beginning to sour into loneliness. I was ready for love. I was tired of having drinks with my coupled friends, radiant in the salt and sunlight of our city, carefully indulgent of me. I found a date, someone with cute glasses and fun hair. We met. We kissed. The details are meaningless, except that he walked like my first love and for that I followed him when I shouldn't have. And when he raped me I said, 'No, no, no', so politely, because I was scared, and confused, and thought I was good at judging people.

Or:

Actually, I *do* know what that's like because it happened to me and fuck you very much for assuming otherwise.

Or:

When the rape happened, which was approximately around the time that Pharrell Williams song 'Happy' was in the charts, ironic isn't it? Anyway…

Or:

Like approximately 47% of bisexual men I have been the victim of a sexual assault.

Or:

I'm fine now. Please don't worry.

When I disclose I am balancing my own needs (not to be laughed at or disbelieved) with the needs of the other person, I cannot trust people to deal well with me as a survivor, because – like Elliot – many people have not.

We know that male friendships are a lynchpin in how our society thinks about sexual violence. There is compelling evidence to suggest that male abusers are more likely to have friendship groups which engage in the kind of misogyny that Elliot confronted me with.[2] We also know that, particularly within a university context, a huge number of people will find themselves offering some level of support to friends who disclose abuse.

What we need in order to do this successfully is mediated by gender:

'Male and female friends of survivors may need to focus on different issues related to being a bystander and ally. Male bystanders may need to build confidence in their abilities to be supportive to friends, whereas female bystanders may need assistance with their own feelings of vulnerability and anxiety that may arise from the bystander role.'[3]

For men like Elliot, that confidence has to be built on education and anti-sexism. And for the other men in my life, many of whom fumbled through their support of me and found my status as a survivor so awkward that they allowed our friendships to lapse, I think that confidence also comes from having the habit of vulnerable discussion, intimate sharing, and trust already built into their friendships.

And here, I'm happy to say, we are making progress. There is a large body of research over the past ten or so years which shows that 'men are engaging in more affectionate, emotional, and physical relationships with their same-sex friends,'[4] with positive impacts on disclosure experiences of all kinds. Researchers attribute this rapid change to the efforts of LGBTQ+ activists and the destigmatisation of homosexuality.[5]

So, it shouldn't surprise me that my first group of mostly-male friends in years came from that community. Twice a month I play Dungeons & Dragons with a group

of queer friends, all of whom have strong ties to masculinity and manhood. We began adventuring together
during lockdown and, rather than cleaving close to the
traditional rule-based D&D model (which involves
an unholy amount of maths), have cut a merry swathe
through various campaigns fuelled largely by the Rule of
Funny. We have laughed each other into paroxysms and
nearly brought our Dungeon Master (sort of a Master
of Ceremonies/chief storyteller) to tears on several occasions. It's just fun. It's the sort of fun I never thought
I would have with male friends – much less men who
knew I was a survivor – ever again.*

Within the LGBTQ+ community the gendered
dimensions of sexual violence are much less stark
than within the general population, but the general
perception of abuse as a 'women's problem' still obscures
the experiences of many men, especially trans men and
non-binary people with strong connections to manhood.
This is a double loss. Firstly, because without listening
to these voices we cannot offer them the safety and
support they deserve and secondly because their stories
offer us valuable information about men's experiences in

---

* It's worth noting that games like Dungeons & Dragons can be an
incredible tool for healing. SurvivorsUK, one of the UK's largest
sexual violence charities which helps men and nonbinary people, is
possibly the only organisation of its kind to keep a Dungeon Master
on staff. Role-playing games like D&D are a form of collaboration,
but they also allow us to explore violence, conflict and safety.

general. No one enters the world as a fully formed man after all, but the trans road to manhood requires far more reflection and intentionality than the cis one.

One study which spoke to trans men sketches out the huge amount of complexity in how they negotiate violence in public. As men transition, generally speaking, they move from a being perceived as part of the demographic safest from non-sexual violence (women, particularly if seen as feminine) to one of the most at risk (men, particularly if seen as feminine). At the same time, the way they interact with this violence changes. Rather than managing threats of violence collectively and being able to take concrete steps to avoid it, as women often do, the corresponding jump in risk is accompanied by a pressure not to express fear. In the UK a countries a man walking home alone is far more likely to be physically attacked than a woman is,[6] but he is also far less likely to have anyone texting him to check that he has arrived back safely. The onus is on him to protect himself, not on the creation of a communal safety.

For most men, the skills to navigate this reality are cultivated in childhood. But for trans men the picture is different. One study notes that, 'Trans men often lack the boyhood experiences common to cisgender men of fighting and learning how to handle non-sexual violence from other men. Thus, they are newly orienting them-selves to being accountable to gender expectations for those who are sex categorized as male.'[7]

The result is that trans men, like their cis brothers, tend to defend against violence to this reality by reinforcing patriarchal behaviours, even when they conflict with their values:

> 'Almost all of the interviewees described wanting to be "good" men and many felt that their defensive practices did not align with the kind of men they desired to be. There was some variation in how they defined being a "good" man, but almost half of interviewees specifically said that this meant they did not support gender hierarchies and detailed ways in which they strived to transform existing gender relations.'[8]

We have tied so much of men's access to safety to the performance of traditional masculinity and the practice of misogyny that it is incredibly high risk for us to leave it behind.

As much as I love and have a lot in common with my male friends, my work means almost constant interaction with women who have experiences of violence. I've spoken before about what we have in common as victims; trauma, anxiety, fear. But sometimes it is more straightforward. Sometimes, we have been harmed by the very same people.

We used to think that offenders kept to one 'type' of victim. It makes for a better story and fits with what we think we know about serial killers and other high profile criminal behaviours. Initially the evidence supported this. However, as our understanding of sexual violence has deepened we are revealing more and more crossover in the behaviour of sex offenders. We have known for example, that when boys are the identified victims of sexual abuse by their fathers, there are additional victims (usually the boys' sisters) in around 60% of cases.[9]

In fact, an emerging picture suggests that 'the age and gender of a victim, and their relationship to an offender, are not considerations for many perpetrators of sexual crime, which challenges assumptions made by traditional means of categorization [sic]'.[10]

This doesn't mean that gender plays no part in these offenders' behaviour, nor that misogyny does not shape their offending and create a disproportionate impact on women and girls. But it does mean that an offender might still target women and girls for reasons which have little to do with his own sexist beliefs and everything to do with practical things like who he has access to, who sexual violence is normalised against, who is less likely to be believed. If his situation changes – for example, if he is convicted of a crime and incarcerated in a men's prison – it is entirely possible that he will simply switch over to offending against other men.[11]

What does this mean for survivor communities? Sexual violence is always a form of gendered attack; in that it shapes and reshapes our experiences of gender. For many it is a radicalising experience. I can imagine that many victims might find it disorientating to think that even though the impact on their sense of gender was significant, it was not a strong motivating factor in the mind of their perpetrator.

One of the things I was sure of after I was raped was that I was not my rapist's first victim. He was simply too slick, too self-assured, too competent. His anticipation of how I would try to push back, how to gaslight me into pretending that everything was fine afterwards and muddy the evidence spoke of a long experience. He was too good at it to not be well practised.

Vaguely, I assumed that the other people he had raped were men. I wanted to believe I wasn't alone, that their experiences were like mine in more ways than the person who harmed us. But the reality is that there's no reason we should be. If I were to imagine a room full of his other victims, it seems more likely that we would be a mixed-gender group. Given that, what might we owe each other as people who have been harmed by the same person? What would my presence as a co-victim do to a woman's sense of her experience as a form of gender-based violence? Anything? Nothing? In the absence of a healthy public dialogue between survivors of all genders this can only be answered through friendships.

In her memoir *Unbroken,* the author, speaker and survivor Madeleine Black describes a counselling client she had, one of her first significant encounters with a male survivor after years of being frightened of men following her own rape.

'I knew that what had helped me most, regardless of the emotional difficulty, was to connect to the pain, to stay with the facts of the event, so I did my best to guide him through that… It moved me so much to see a man cry in the way he did that often my eyes filled up too. I suddenly saw this man as another human being who had been hurt and was no different to me or anyone else. From that moment on, my opinion of men was altered and I saw them as my equals rather than enemies or people to be feared.'[12]

Black's experience is her own and everyone who has survived male violence has a different way of relating to male survivors as a group. But one way or another we do relate to each other. And, for me, it changes things when I imagine that the women and non-binary survivors in my life might, for all I know, have been harmed by the same perpetrator as me.

The simple truth is that it matters to me what these women might think of me. Imagining their existence, their experiences, the way they might be living now, reliably brings up a warm, complex feeling. It is solidarity, connection, it is a hope that they will be happy. I worry about them in the same way that I worry about friends on their way home from the club, or loved ones who don't call after a flight. And, perhaps selfishly, bizarrely, it hurts to think that they might not worry about me. That they might never even pause to imagine my existence or that they might be indifferent to it. I'd be lying if I said I knew why I feel this way, but I don't.

But what I do know for sure is that this feeling is a stronger emotional base to begin the work of male allyship than any other I have access to. It is more real and more galvanising than male guilt, or anger at the way that many men act, or the desire to be seen as a good person. Every survivor is different, and gender is a big difference, but there is a sense in which I feel closer to these women than I do to some of the people I really know. When I have been able to challenge sexism and misogyny in the moment, when I have pushed myself over the awkwardness and intimidation, it has never been because I want to 'do the right thing'. Maybe that should be enough, but it's not. Instead, the thing which tips me over into action is feeling for that connection, that relationship, and reminding myself that staying silent is betraying those people who have suffered under the same hands as I have.

Under our current way of thinking about men's role in anti-violence work, though, it can be incredibly difficult to harness this feeling. Many of the men's spaces I've encountered struggle with what to do with male survivors. They fear that spending time on violence against men risks derailing their stated goals of de-centring men's voices and experiences. In practice though, this means that male survivors who feel as I do, deeply committed to ensuring our collective safety, can feel pressured to hide our experiences. I have found myself pretending I am not a survivor, performing an ignorance of the impacts of sexual trauma and even feeling guilty for being triggered by descriptions of sexual violence. As a result, my own efforts at preventing gender based harm have stayed individual and sporadic, rather than consistent and structural. I cannot yet find a way to bring my whole self to the communities doing this kind of work, because they are asking me not to.

The relationships men have with anti-sexist work are always going to involve difficulty, and I think it's worth looking at what motivates us in order to stay with that difficulty. I am increasingly convinced that the idea of 'allyship' is insufficient to the task. It's a formal, military and strategic term which doesn't sit comfortably in most of our lives. It implies distance and, while it does a good job at recognising that we all have different levels of skin in the game, it also feels remote. Where 'allyship' often feels like I am being hemmed in, forced to lop off or suppress parts of myself, 'friendship' often opens things out.

As a friend, putting someone else's needs first feels like a gift, like an investment into an ongoing relationship, like a flow of give and take and mutual flourishing which is more rooted in who I want to be. My friendship with M, and with other women and non-binary people in my life, are the places where I am most capable of the kind of active listening, holding space, offering support and acknowledging differences of experience and privilege. They are the places where I can care wholly and authentically about someone else's interests, and take real joy in their successes, where I can make mistakes and keep returning, apologise; where standing up for them feels instinctive, and where we have permission to be imperfect. We know what we're like as friends. We know what we have to offer to a friendship.

The week after Sarah Everard was murdered I was due to co-facilitate a peer support session for other survivor-activists and, like most of these spaces, we were expecting a largely female cohort. As the day approached, I grew increasingly unsure what my role in the space would be like in the context of a very clear and traumatic form of male violence. I didn't know what the 'allyship' looked like and I felt I had very little time to figure it out. So, I went to 'friendship' instead. I could see that many of the women I would be holding space for were angry; they wanted to vent, and act, and mourn, and say how pissed off they were. As a friend, I'm good at holding space for that, I've done it when my friends are bereaved.

So, I offered the organisers an extra hour of my time for us to hold some space and just allow the women there to gather beyond the formal, action-based session. We prepared some prompts and safeguards just in case the levels of emotion went beyond our ability to hold, but by and large we just wanted to ask how people were. It was the scaled up, organisational equivalent of calling up a friend to say, 'Hey, I can imagine you're going through it right now. I'm happy to help with the practical stuff as it emerges, but do you need to just talk?'

The feedback was that the session worked. It wasn't perfect and it certainly wasn't comfortable, but it was necessary. It was also much easier to recognise the unique feelings that women, particularly women of colour, in my community had around the response to Sarah Everard's murder.

Working from a place of political friendship created a sense of emotional abundance. I knew it was okay for me to not be at the centre of this discussion right now, but there would be time later if I needed it. I could feel my silence not as repression, but a form of listening. It also allowed me to approach the session as my whole self. I was not trying to be the platonic ideal of the 'male ally',

I was just me, offering what I could and looking out for the people I love.

I believe we need to stop thinking as allies and move towards a scaled up, politicised movement of friendship. If you are the kind of person who offers your skills to a friend in need then why not do so to organisations which look after their interests? If you bring around sandwiches to a friend going through bereavement, then why not offer material support to those who are mourning the loss of their rights, safety and agency?

If we can do this it might give male, female, and non-binary survivors a framework for the kind of flexible collaboration we need to truly make a difference. The road to an equal world involves wading through the complex skeins of privilege, power and positionality that shape our society. And it is through friendship that we do that best.

Chapter 3
Fathers

'If you're ever adopting, leave the abuse business out. I'm speaking as a social worker here.'

My stomach flipped over.

A little after I did my first piece of public facing work about my experience of rape, a friend was talking about it. She said how refreshing it was, and how hopeful it made her to see male vulnerability being modelled by a young person. Our conversation twisted and turned in that delightful way that conversations with people who are giddy in the face of big ideas do. She was a mental health nurse and before that a social worker, with deep and practical insights into the human mind. But it is this warning that struck me.

I already knew what she meant. The Vampire Myth, the idea that men who have been sexually assaulted are fated to go on and become perpetrators ourselves, is one which we all have to navigate sooner or later, and it particularly affects queer men who come into contact with children. I'd already heard stories like this; male nurses steered discreetly away from paediatric care, male booksellers deftly kept out of the children's section.

The idea that by speaking out about my rape I had compromised my ability to have children was stomach turning at the time. Now, as my thirties loom, it has mellowed into a niggling dread. I turn over the possibility of fatherhood in my head, scared to want it in case no one will allow me to have it if I should ask.

I'm not unusual in this. One of the few things we know about male survivors is that we are more likely to give up on the possibility of fatherhood – disproportionately compared to female survivors' attitudes to motherhood.[1]

One of the questions I am often asked is, 'How should we encourage male survivors to speak up more?' The easy answer, which I've often given, is about tackling 'toxic masculinity', a term which in this context people almost always interpret as meaning 'men's harmful beliefs about what it means to be a man, which keep them too ashamed to speak out or seek help.' This is part of the picture, but it's not the whole explanation. It is very easy and comfortable for us to put male silence down to the psychology of the sufferer. It is less easy, less comfortable, for us to examine the social forces which keep men silent, even when they are ready to speak up.

These are more practical concerns than emotional. Men, like any other survivors, weigh the potential benefits of seeking help against the costs to themselves and their loved ones; a calculation which is almost entirely about navigating their societal roles. For example, in the aftermath of conflict based sexual violence in the Democratic Republic of the Congo (DRC), Nigeria, many male survivors highlighted the risk of revictimisation; intuiting correctly that men who are known to be survivors are more likely to be targeted again by other perpetrators.[2]

Given this picture, that men who speak out about sexual violence are more likely to be assaulted again and face unfair scrutiny as potential sex offenders and have a harder time becoming dads in the first place, is it any wonder that many men seem to see speaking out about their abuse and having children as mutually exclusive? Certainly, in my circles all but one of the out male survivors I've worked with have been childless.

This is another area where the research is patchy, but what we do know is that male survivors who do become fathers spend a lot of time navigating the Vampire Myth, either because they believe it, or because they are frightened that other people do.

The day after the rape I threw myself into my tutor's office and told her what happened. She reacted with such empathy and compassion that I still say that every survivor deserves one of her. She arranged for me to have counselling through my university, and it was there that I encountered the Vampire Myth.

'I'm scared I'll hurt someone if I let myself recover,' I said to my counsellor.

'Do you mean you're having violent thoughts?' Her voice was impressively even.

'No, I don't want to hurt anyone. I'm afraid I just will.'

'Okay. So you're afraid your anger will get out of control or...?'

'No.' I hadn't had a single angry thought or impulse since the rape. In fact, anger seemed hermetically sealed off from my personality.

'So why are you afraid you'll hurt someone?'

'I don't know, I don't know, I don't know, I just am.'

At this point my frustration spilled over into a panic attack. This woman, this calm bespectacled woman with a sunny office, simply didn't understand. I felt like I had been infected.

I thought that in some way the rape had put male violence inside me. I had to be vigilant, super vigilant, against it, or I would inevitably perpetrate it because, well, isn't that what abused men did? I felt, and it's no exaggeration to say this, like I was a monster in waiting. I tried to explain this to my counsellor, and she looked confused.

'I'm not sure I understand,' she said. 'If you don't want to sexually assault someone, you don't have to. You can choose not to.'

It was less like a penny dropping, and more like the cascade of change in one of the arcade machines on the end of Brighton Pier.

On the one hand I was relieved. I was not fundamentally broken. The rape was not because I was, in some way, bad or a lightning rod for sex offenders. What had happened to me was not just sad, it was actually wrong.

On the other hand I was disturbed; I had to confront the fact that my rapist had chosen to harm me, just as I had the power to choose not to harm other people. It made it, somehow, more personal. I also had to confront the fact that this was *not* the picture I'd gotten from various professionals who dealt with me in the immediate aftermath of the rape, who had treated me as an annoyance.

But it was true. Rape happens because people make a choice to commit it. It sounds so utterly basic, and yet everything I had been shown and taught in my life as a man about why sex offences happen was upended in that single moment.

My counsellor looked me over in that attentive way they have, as though they are trying to broadcast empathy like a search beam out of their eyeballs.

'Oh,' I said. 'I hadn't really thought of that.'

I confronted the Vampire Myth in the wake of my rape at the hands of a man, but research suggests it's even stronger for men who are the victims of female perpetrators. One small study of Icelandic survivor-fathers found that:

'The fear of abusing their children was so strong that several participants reported spending less time with their children or avoided being alone with them. Survivors also reported feeling afraid of touching their children, bathing or toileting their daughters, or playing contact games with their sons for fear of causing inappropriate arousal in either the child or themselves'.[3]

We need to remember that these are not men who have any particular history of inappropriate arousal or abusive behaviours but are nonetheless treating themselves as high risk purely as a result of internalising the myth that tells them they will be. We can imagine the impact this might have on children; making them feel as though their fathers are distant or unloving, and on these men's (mainly female) partners; making them responsible for caring responsibilities around hygiene for their children.

We know that these emotional responses are remarkably similar to those of survivor-mothers, who have tended to report lack of connection and overprotect-iveness in their experiences of parenthood.[4] But we don't yet have a clear idea of how different social attitudes to motherhood and fatherhood shape the impact of these emotions in survivors' lives.

From the outside, we can see how these men's behaviour might be interpreted through the classic model of negligent, patriarchal and traditional attitudes to parenthood; the idea that caring labour is down to the mothers. And yet these survivor-fathers are doing an enormous amount of emotional work here. The constant policing of their own feelings, the active shutting down of the desire to be close to one's own children – these take colossal and invisible effort. It says something damning about our society that we have taught these fathers that silence and absence are the best thing they can offer their children.

And for male survivors in the Global South, at least, there may be precious little else they can offer which falls into the traditional provider role that fathers usually occupy. Data from the DRC and other areas which see high levels of male victimisation in conflict show a clear link between sexual abuse of male victims in conflict and economic hardship, poverty and low growth for their entire communities, noting:

'Some parents, and especially young boys who have not yet encountered sexual violence, are in persistent fear that they might be the next victims. This deters them from going to the mines, rearing animals in the fields, planting crops, and harvesting produce for the market. The loss of livelihoods occasioned by extreme insecurity as a result of the threat of sexual violence has made many men and boys vulnerable. Many males can no longer go about their normal duties for fear of being attacked.'[5]

In the DRC particularly, the fear of revictimisation has been noted as a major factor pushing men out of the workforce.[6] That means an increased risk that their families will wind up experiencing poverty and deprivation with all that entails. Fathers experience this as an urgent, unshakeable loss of self. As one man put it, 'There is nothing worse than this life.'[7]

The questions I have as a man, living in the Global North, currently childless and with conflicting feelings about fatherhood, are difficult to answer. We have very little understanding of how the male survivor experience impacts fatherhood over the course of the parenting journey. I want to know what it might be like to have a new-born waking me up in the middle of the night, to have discussions with my potential teen and pre-teen kids about sex. What will happen if, one day, they decide to google me and find the details of my rape?

More than that, if I have children with a future female partner, or if women are involved in assisted fertility, adoption or other forms of family-making also happen to be survivors, how might our experiences interact? What about IVF and/or surrogacy? The last time I dealt with anything sexual in a doctor's surgery was the forensic examination after my rape and subsequent sexual health screenings. How on earth would I ever manage masturbating into a cup on demand in a similar context, and what happens if I simply *can't?* What is it even like for a child to grow up in a household where both their primary caregivers are survivors?

Connie Walker's investigative podcast, *Silenced: Surviving Saint Michaels,* is one of the few accounts we have of what it is like to be the child of a survivor-father. Walker's father was abused by a priest during his childhood at a 'residential school' in Canada, one of the Canadian government's attempts to disrupt indigenous communities by indoctrinating their children into Catholicism. He later grew up to be a police officer and she describes a chance meeting between the two men on a silent, isolated road in rural Saskatchewan.

'My dad was driving alone in his patrol car when he spotted a set of tail lights swerving ahead in the darkness. He flicked on his lights and the car pulled over on the side of the road.'

Walker imagines the confrontation that occured between her father and his former abuser, during which the priest was beaten practically to a pulp.

'My dad walked back to his patrol car and drove off into the night, leaving the man crumpled on the side of the road. There were no witnesses. The only people who knew what really happened were the two men who were there. But this is how I imagine the story. It's a story that my father told that was later told to me. Hearing it has changed the way I think about my life.'[8]

Listening to Walker describe her father is an encounter with a violent, angry man. Someone whose rage spills into creating an unsafe environment for her as a child. But her brother and younger siblings remember their late father very differently; as a man who was patient and gentle with his children, who taught them important things, who was able to give some voice to his experiences of abuse. When she interviews her brother, we find two siblings experiencing the full spectrum of what survivor fathers can be like. Walker's brother feels pride at his father's story about beating up his former abuser, but Walker immediately imagines the boy her father was.

I feel bizarrely paternal listening to these two siblings discussing the legacies of colonial abuse on their father.

Both are older than I am, and yet I imagine the complexities they deal with are similar to those that my potential children might also need to talk about, around a firepit someday in a possible future. I am struck by how they replay the imagined face of the priest, turning over trauma memories they do not even have with the same attention that I turn over my own. Walker's father gave her nightmares that I recognised.

Walker notes in the podcast that she has investigated residential schools for some time. She knew her dad was in one, but never joined the dots. Few people do – asking whether our fathers have been sexually assaulted is uncomfortable, and if I'm honest, too close to my own experience to ignore. Like me, Walker has a father who is full of unanswered questions and odd volatilities. Though continents apart, both attended Catholic boarding schools which had the express purpose of brutalising them out of their own indigenous cultures. Both had tempers which loomed large in the psyches of their children, and while my father made obvious and passionate attempts to control his temper, it did put me into harm's way. As Walker says, 'Despite the lingering effects of his anger on my life, I've never fully understood where that came from in him.'[9]

Describing their brother near the end of his life, Walker's aunts paint a picture of a man who was gentle with his younger children and nearly unrecognisable from the father who Walker knew. He had managed to release the anger which endangered his family, but not in time to prevent it damaging his relationship with his eldest daughter.

In her podcast, Walker uses the revelation that her dad was abused as a portal for revisiting her relationship with him after his death. It's part of her inheritance, and it seems it wasn't passed down to her in the best shape. On uncovering the abuse with her aunts, she says, 'It feels amazing on one hand because I feel like I'm remembering a part of myself with every conversation…but then it's also just so sad because my dad passed away and the only way I can get to know him now is through these interviews and these conversations with people who knew him better than I did. My dad was stolen from me because his childhood was stolen from him by residential school, but also by a man in a black robe.'[10]

If I ever am a father, I know I would like to be remembered the way Walker's younger siblings remember their dad – as someone with patience and kindness and someone who kept them safe. I think most men, survivors or not, would say the same. But there is still part of me which worries that having children will change who I am for the worse. Parenthood is a consistent risk factor for the worsening of PTSD or other trauma related disorders, with fathers most affected. One large study found that fathers who lived with their children were 40% more likely to develop PTSD than childless or estranged fathers.[11] I have never had an especially violent or aggressive response to my own trauma, but I can see clearly how my own patterns of avoidance, withdrawal and acquiescence might be devastating for my own children. Will that be what happens? Can I overcome it if it does? Who will help me if I can't do it alone?

Those are just my questions, particular to my body, my time of life, my experience and expectations of fatherhood. But there are so many male experiences and contexts. One colleague who works with male survivors tells me that watching a partner go through pregnancy and birth can be incredibly triggering for some men who have had their relationships with women exploited as part of their abuse. If an abuser has told a young boy that his mother or sisters will be hurt if he doesn't stay silent then the spectacle of a woman he loves in extreme pain can result in a massive trauma reaction right at the moment when he is most needed to be dependable and supportive.

And that's just traditional fatherhood. We know next to nothing at the data level about, for example, transgender survivor-fathers who have to navigate a whole suite of conflicting medical landscapes. We know very little about how disabled survivor-fathers navigate social expectations of the strong, stable protector with an inviolable body and the attendant ableisms this image brings. We know next to nothing about how gay and bisexual men, migrant men, neurodivergent men and many, many other groups manage the confluences of fatherhood and survivorhood. Time and again in researching this chapter, more than any other, I have run into the dreaded words of an academic dead end – 'more research is required.'

Parenthood is always something of a leap into darkness, but it does not seem unreasonable to ask society to offer us a few stars to light the way. Here the research lets us down badly. So many of us are the unknowing children of male survivors and may have had our early lives radically changed by that inheritance. And yet we remain institutionally incurious about it. Why?

I don't know if I will have children. There are so many other questions that I need to answer before I am ready to decide one way or the other whether it's a good idea. But the idea of parenting in a world where sexual violence can barrel into your life, unexpected and in an instant, is a terrifying one. I am afraid that my trauma will paralyse me in the moments that matter, that the resulting mental illness will make it hard to do all the things that parents have to do. I'm worried that as a man who would rather be an involved and active parent I will be held to high standards and found wanting. I am frightened that my children might experience the same kinds of violence I have experienced, and that my own trauma will get in the way of supporting them if they do. And I am coldly furious that my rapist's actions may have compromised my potential to be a good parent.

I'm not angry very often, not even at people who have harmed me. But I am angry about that. I am angry in a deep down, festering, inexpressible way that feels like a scream I have been holding in for the best part of ten years. A scream which nobody would think important or understand, that I am expected simply to swallow.

But there is some hope. In the few studies that do tackle survivor-fatherhood there is a theme which recurs; that of fatherhood as a healing experience. In a 2012 review of the literature on dads recovering from childhood sexual abuse I found the following quote:

> 'I look at my children and I say "hey this is me, if I stripped back the abuse this is who I am, I am like these kids, I am good, I am positive, I can believe in myself, I can do things, I can explore the world." I guess that's probably it in that sort of sense. I am lucky to have four great kids and to be able to just be with them and allow them to teach me.'[12]

The review goes on to examine the positive role that parenting in this way; with presence, flexibility and humility, can play in men's recoveries from sexual trauma.

Far from making them a risk factor, some male survivors use their experiences as fuel for an engaged parenting style, determined to make sure their children do not have the same experiences they did of being silenced.

Our best hope of catalysing these positive visions of fatherhood are to tell better stories about (and with) survivor dads. Researchers in a 2018 study of survivor fathers found that, 'A narrative approach to therapy embraces the idea of fatherhood as an opportunity for fathers to assume a new narrative, one that is based on competence, growth, and emotional connection rather than on pathology, fear and isolation.'[13]

In 2021, I joined a Zoom call with a small group of men who were discussing avenues for sharing their stories and supporting other survivors. One person was in a music studio. Another was at his kitchen table. And another was in his bedroom, the camera facing his bed. And behind him, doing her homework, was his daughter. We did the work we were doing. Every now and again he would glance back, just slightly, just to check on her. He spoke smoothly, clearly, openly about the fact that he was a survivor. I squinted to see whether she was wearing headphones. No. She could hear. Twice she asked him a question and he muted, threw an answer over his shoulder in that absent-minded way parents do, and returned back to his work. She went back to her homework.

It sounds like such a small moment, but I was seeing something most of us never see. I had never, ever seen a man managing to be both a father and a visible survivor. Something released inside me; that scream of anger faltered for the first time. There, in front of me on the screen, was a small window into a possible future.

One that should be on the table for all of us.

Chapter 4
Lovers

Six months before I was raped, I moved into a new place, a tiny studio flat in Brighton, just enough room for a sofa bed, bookcase and desk, plus a little shared garden out back. It was cramped and mouldy; halfway through my tenancy the back door came off and I had to wedge it shut. But it was all mine.

I bought little bundles of Sweet William from the organic grocer on the corner, split them between two vases and set about figuring out my sex life. I'd spent most of the prior two years in relationships which were more-or-less monogamous and the rest of the time having fairly unfulfilling one-night stands. I wanted neither now. Being a Black teenager in an almost exclusively white environment had had taught me a lot that I needed to unlearn. I slowly began to believe that I was not ugly, that I deserved to be more than an experiment for the straight white women and gay men who were happy to have sex with me until someone better (read: paler, more masculine, handsomer) came along. For the first time in my life, I made a list of what I wanted out of my sex life.

1. Variety. I was used to being roundly rejected for being bisexual. If I was going to be stereotyped as slutty and voracious, I might as well actually *do* it. More importantly I enjoyed the idea of sex with people who expressed and understood gender in radically different ways. I liked watching different parts of my own sexuality respond, recede, adapt. I enjoyed being changed by who I was fucking. So, ideally the opportunity to sleep with men, women, non-binary people and couples.

2. Consistency. My favourite part of sex was always the bit that felt like learning. Finding out exactly what made my partner tick, the trial and error of learning someone's body. Sex was best when it was permission to be fascinated with someone else's pleasure. Plus, I was an awful first shag. It takes me at least two or three sessions to properly relax enough to show someone a good time. Or, as one of my partners put it: 'Bloody hell, have you always actually been that good at that?'

3. Companionship. I didn't want a relationship but going to bed with people I didn't like always felt pointless. If I wouldn't have dinner with them, I wouldn't sleep with them.

4. Communication. I was absolutely done with the mysterious semi-relationships which began with all the enthusiasm of a chemical reaction and then fizzled out like bath foam. Clarity, boundaries, and lots of humour were what I needed.

All things considered I did very well. I approached a few people I'd already slept with, went on a few other dates, and slowly put together a rotation of regular lovers; two single men, a woman, an opposite sex couple and a gay couple, plus a cadre of other bisexual nerds who were primarily friends but occasionally fell into bed with me. Mostly, it worked. Apart from the odd hiccup where one of my lover's other lovers was diagnosed with glandular fever, I managed to juggle this set up pretty successfully.

This is the context in which I was raped that February morning. It was devastating, obviously, but it was also exhausting to think that all the work I had done to unpick my own insecurities, to build a sex life built on consent, communication and joy, could be wiped out in an instant. That by the actions of a single, selfish person, my life could be upended. I was more ashamed than when I was a teenager figuring out I was bi, more objectified than the boy on the bus being asked how big his penis was. And as I surfaced from the trauma of that experience I realised something. I would have to tell all of the people I was sleeping with what had happened. Or at least some version of it.

Disclosing to a partner, whether a casual partner or a long-term prospect, is one of the most vulnerable moments that male survivors face. In a post #MeToo world, many male survivors find themselves in relationships with female partners who are becoming more and more outspoken about their own experiences, and their response is often bittersweet.

'I'm so proud of her,' one such man said to me at a party. We were both about five ciders from sensible conversation and I'd told him what I did or a living. It was good to see his pride. He'd spent a good deal of the evening boasting about how his girlfriend was pushing for her workplace and industry to take sexual harassment of women seriously, to implement proper policies, to invest real money in equality and change their organisational structures. Earlier, the way he spoke held a fierce, intimate admiration. Now though, as the alcohol hit his system, something else emerged.

I won't go into detail about the forms of abuse he disclosed to me, but it's enough to know that his girlfriend's work was, in some ways, profoundly upsetting. When she came home enraged or despondent at the patriarchal machine her frustration would ignite his own trauma. Fear would surface, to which his response was to freeze up and become uncommunicative. Her frustration grew as she read this as a lack of support or even complicity in rape culture. And so they were caught in a feedback loop.

'I'm scared if I start talking about the stuff she's doing too much I'll let it slip. Or she'll suspect. She's clever and she'll suspect.'

'Would that be so bad? Couldn't you tell her?' I asked.

His answer was a violent, shuddering shake of the head.

'She's dealing with so much already,' he said, admiration and despair slurring together in his voice. 'There's no room. That's how it feels. Like there's so much of her trauma that there's no room for mine.'

It was a long night. At one point he sobbed in my arms, at another we laughed together at the worst excesses of our teenage music taste (mine, My Chemical Romance; his, Mumford and Sons). I messaged the next day to offer a listening ear, but he never responded. I think he didn't want to feel like a burden.

It would be easy for me to say that he should have spoken to his girlfriend, and that there is no shame in being a survivor. But this man was not silent out of shame. He was silent out of love. The same respect and pride that led him to champion his girlfriend's activism was preventing him from being truly open with her. Whether or not this is the right approach for him to take, it's worth asking whether he is completely wrong in his assessment of what disclosing would mean for his relationship. In a context where services for male survivors are patchy it is entirely possible that his girlfriend, as a woman with some expertise in the area of sexual trauma, would wind up shouldering a disproportionate amount of the work of supporting him. Her own activism might well suffer as a result.

Both research and practice have shown that trauma can be contagious, and we know that women with male partners are particularly susceptible to 'catching' their partner's symptoms. They can find themselves experiencing anger, sleeplessness and hypervigilance that their partners may not even acknowledge.[1] Researchers into this phenomenon suggest that the solution is not really to be found within the couple at all.

'FPs [female partners], MPs [male partners], and their children experience significant distress due to MP CSA. Traditionally, therapists have focused on assisting CSA survivors, giving relatively less attention to CSA's systemic effects (Bacon & Lein, 1996). Individual interventions for survivors should be supplemented with couples and family counseling [sic].'[2]

This recommendation relies on a mental health infrastructure which we are still building, one which does not confine the treatment of male survivors to specialists within sexual violence services, but which takes the sexual abuse of men as a serious issue within the context of couples and family counselling. It also needs to acknowledge that women and non-binary people, both groups with specialist needs, might find interacting with these stories difficult. We need an architecture of mental health support which can hold all of these things in balance and support couples of all kinds.

In the absence of that architecture, silence might be the best tool at our disposal.

The man I met at the party was, in many other ways, a very privileged person. He was white and English, from the South East. He was straight, cisgender and with no visible disabilities. He lived in the West with citizenship of a Western country. But if we look further afield, we begin to see other contexts in which male survivors might be forced to stay silent as a tool to maintain relationships with their partners.

Sexual violence against men has been used as a weapon of war many contexts, including in Bosnia, Kenya and Uganda. In the wake of the latter, where government forces sexually assaulted men often in public, at the same time as their female family members, or in front of their whole communities, one of the consequences was a huge increase in family breakdown. The idea that these men had been emasculated was so profound that many of them found themselves being blamed when their wives experienced miscarriage, difficulty conceiving, or even for the deaths of their children in infancy.[3] These women often leave their husbands, in part because they are aware that they are no longer seen as protector figures, and as such they feel vulnerable to increased victimisation by sexual predators. Safer, they calculate, to be alone.

But there is also a more complex attitude that some of these women have towards their husbands, and it's one which I struggle to approach neutrally. Many women simply don't want a male survivor as a husband because they find it unsatisfying. They do not want husbands who experience sexual dysfunction, and men from these communities do report their wives participating in the kind of shaming that we know can be so destructive. The fact that their husband's assaults and the ensuing disabilities often pushes these women into survival sex work or puts them in the way of sexual harm. We can imagine how easily they might grow to resent the men closest to them.

Men of Hope are a male survivors' organisation in Kampala who support refugees from conflict zones all over Africa. In their most recent report they recommend, among other things, that partners and families be invited into the orbit of service providers so that the couples can tackle the legacies of sexual violence together.[4]

This is just one way that sexual violence against men sits within and influences the broader context of violence against women and girls. And as horrific as this particular situation was, it shows us the necessity of transforming how we intervene in gender-based violence as a whole. It's clear how patriarchal ideas and misogyny facilitated this violence. But an intervention which was only interested in female victims would never be able to predict, let alone change, the patterns of violence against women in that particular context. Instead, we needed to widen out to see what was going on in more detail.

Within the sexual violence sector, we often talk about having a gendered lens on these issues, and the need to centre women's views and experiences. But centring those views does not mean zooming in so tightly on them that we exclude everything else. We need a wider lens; one which begins with listening to women but is not afraid to journey out into other perspectives and patterns.

And when we begin to do this, the tapestry of global violence comes into focus in new ways. For example, in the UK around half of men who were murdered for interpersonal reasons were killed by their wife or girlfriend's former abuser.[5] In fact, this is the leading interpersonal connection between victim and murderer. We're not sure how these situations play out exactly, but it seems likely that these are examples of women who have successfully escaped domestic violence, rebuilt their lives and then invited new, safe male partners into them. What this data suggests is that male abusers are literally killing off supportive men in order to make women's lives worse. Based on this data, we can estimate that an average at least one man per week is murdered in such circumstances.[6]

All political violence speaks, and this is clearly political violence. So what does it say? If there is a death toll associated with being a supportive, safe partner to a female survivor then to what extent are men being warned off? Aren't women being told that they will never be safe, that even if they find relationships they're worthy of they will never know peace of mind? What is this violence communicating, not just to the victims, but to our society?

In at least one case, we don't have to guess because the perpetrators have told us.

In 'Male on Male Rape', one of the earliest anthologies of male survivor scholarship, the activist Russ Irving Fink details an experience he had while delivering anti-racism and anti-rape workshops for men in a small town in the southern United States. While attempting to create a space in which white men were challenged on the misogynist and racist structures they were upholding, Fink was gang raped by a group of local men. 'During the attack,' he writes,[7] 'they made several references to the workshop and presentations I had offered in the community: "How can you talk about stopping rape when you can't even stop your own?'

Fink's maleness did not shield him from patriarchal violence, which easily sacrifices male bodies as collateral damage if they become too threatening. But his generosity in sharing it helps us ask better questions. For example: is violence between men motivated by misogyny a hate crime? Should it be? Whose job is it to protect men who might be targeted because of their feminist actions and beliefs? Leaving these questions unanswered typically means delegating the work of ensuring justice and support to those with the fewest resources to do it.

*

In the two weeks after the rape I was, more or less, dead from the neck down and repulsed by the thought of sex. I could barely bear to touch my body in the shower or when going to the toilet. There was absolutely no way I could go to bed with anyone.

This isn't the only response. Plenty of survivors dive into their sex lives post assault. It's often a way of reclaiming control or acting out the assault in hope of a different conclusion. This is so common, in fact, that hypersexual behaviour in children is typically considered a sign that they may have been abused.[8]

Not so for me. I fled my sexuality like someone jumping out of a burning aircraft. The first text from one of my lovers, innocently inviting me over, sent me straight into a dangerous panic attack during which I couldn't walk past the kitchen knives in fear of hurting myself. I simply couldn't deal with hearing from any of the others.

How do you let your lovers know you have been raped? I decided to text them, the greeting card industry having missed this niche. I sat, curled up in my flat in the small gap between my bed and the window, agonising over the wording, tone, level of detail.

I had no idea whether my interest in sex would ever return, or what it would look like if it did. Was it fair to say I'd be back again in another month? Six? I also didn't know whether I'd contracted HIV or not. I didn't know if I would want to see any of them ever again.

I sent the texts. And for some of those people that was the last time I would hear from them. Because by the time I was interested in sex again I was already falling in love.

The friend who introduced me to my boyfriend was a friend of my Opposite Twin who studied astrophysics. Nowadays she's a vicar, but back then she wore nipple tassels under a blue sequined blazer and threw the most fantastic parties in a succession of student flats. Actually, I suppose it shouldn't surprise me that vicars were big fans of sequined blazers and nipple tassels. The things you hear about the Church of England.

I'd always assumed that the perk of being a literature nerd was proximity to sexy people. Didn't Arthur Miller manage to marry Marilyn Monroe? Aren't authors, with their black polo necks and long words, irresistibly sexy? It turns out, not really. Literary sorts will talk about sex until the cows come home, sure. But if you want an actual orgy, make sure to invite engineers and physicists. The people I met at L's parties were deeply sexy and deeply silly at the same time.

At L's house you'd arrive at nine and pop your bottle into the communal stash. The drinks there were always eclectic; sloe gin and Hungarian liqueurs and absinthe, the real kind, smuggled in by someone's uncle. There was good food too. Sometimes I'd arrive early and we'd spend the afternoon building elaborate pies out of filo pastry or macerating strawberries in gin.

If you were attending the party then the done thing was to drift in early in the evening. No cool points for being fashionably late. You'd chat. If there were too many computer science students, the conversation would drift alarmingly towards the intolerable. I once spent two hours listening to an argument against the existence of time zones. But apart from that, the people were interesting, earnest, passionately geeky about this or that topic. If there is something sexier than competence and enthusiasm, I have yet to find it.

Not everyone at these parties was casually sexual, but a lot of people were. We'd find ourselves in a room, or on a particular sofa. I don't even know if I had that much sex during that time, I mostly remember people's hands on my body, being touched. We make so much in our culture of intense sexuality, but the casual, social sort is gorgeous too. No pressure to escalate, a quick fumble doesn't have to be an overture to something more. So much easier to slide a smile across the coffee table and have the rest of your friends rearrange themselves to put you closer to the object of your affection. So much more convenient, too, to be able to excuse yourself to the kitchen if you're not up to play, passing the unwanted attention on to somebody else in the group who'd like it better.

Sometimes people freaked out. It was fine. One of their lovers would sit and hold them while another slipped to the kitchen for a cup of tea and some baked goods. The door would be shut or open as they wished. If it was open then people might drift in and form a cuddle pile, arms and legs intertwined.

In my mind, these parties are like dreams; warmth, raw edged fabric, plastic Halloween axes, kink, rum, love, touch touch touch. There were squabbles and disagreements, and a truly heart stopping moment when someone was diagnosed with glandular fever and we thought we'd all be laid up for months. Once, it emerged that someone coming to the parties was a sexual predator, though he was thankfully edged out. It wasn't perfect, but it was differently flawed, and sometimes that's enough.

This is what it was like when K and I met. That night there was a birthday cake shaped like a teddy bear and soaked in spirits. We shared a midnight blue sofa in the front room and woke up, cloth mouthed, in the morning, curled into each other. I liked waking up next to him, and I knew I wanted to do it as often as I could.

Sometimes he can't sleep because of my kicking. Of all the consequences of the rape, this is another one which makes me angry. That my rapist's actions are still evident in the bags under my partner's eyes, that I am carrying his actions inside me. The waking symptoms I can control or communicate through. But the nightmares carry me away, unwilling, and so much like the rape itself.

Within the LGBTQ+ community, male survivors of sexual violence are shockingly common. Data from the both the UK[9] and the USA demonstrate that a queer man is about as likely as not to be a survivor. In fact, the odds are that most couples where one party is a queer man will have a survivor in the mix. Given that reality, the lack of discussion of sexual trauma in queer men's media, sex education and relational support is severely lacking.

And yet we don't do badly, all things considered. In *Boys and Sex,* researcher Peggy Orenstein notes that GBT+ men are much more likely to have conversations about pleasure and consent than their straight, cisgender peers.[10] This is despite the legacy of anti-homosexuality laws which shaped gay culture's attitudes to sex; an atmosphere where verbal enthusiastic consent could get you arrested and it was safer to play in silence and ambiguity.

Still, there is a long way to go. One old colleague started a charity out of his bedroom after being raped as a teenager. He used to joke that he kept the lights off during sex not because he was ashamed of his body, but because he didn't want his partners to see the stacks of leaflets about sexual violence he kept next to his bed.

'Even if they're lovely about it, it's not exactly a turn on, is it?' he said.

'No,' I said. 'But it must be a great way of getting them to fuck off the morning after.'

'Assuming you want them to,' he said, with the grin of a man who has reached a stage of life where he'd rather like someone to stay in and cuddle with on a Tuesday evening.

Sexual violence against GBT+ men can come from both inside and outside our community, which means that creating a feeling of safety can be tricky. But given our history; HIV/AIDS advocacy, the astonishing achievements of the safe sex initiatives in the '90s, and other gains, I believe we are one of the communities best equipped to hold space for difficult conversations. We have tons of practice and, as in fashion, the rest of the world will probably follow in our wake. But we need to face the reality that there is no version of healthy LGBT+ sexuality that does not involve tangling with the trauma of sexual violence; either against us or our partners, which the vast majority of us will encounter in some form. What that looks like will be different for everyone. For me, it began like this.

When K and I first got together, I knew I had to tell him what had happened to me. I had absolutely no clue about the future. I had no clue whether I was capable of a relationship, whether I was loveable, whether I would one day begin crying in the middle of sex or develop a clutch of unexpected fetishes or even whether I would be able to have a sexual relationship ever again.

The first time he took me back to his place in West London, I nearly turned around and left. He lived in a basement flat; the same kind as my rape had happened in. I very carefully held my face together, even though it felt like a Picasso underneath, and went down the stairs. *If his bed frame is the same as the rapist's, I am leaving,* I told myself. *I will simply make my excuses and go.*

But it didn't. And the sheets were green, which was also different, and there were lots of the clever little electronics he makes on a desk by the window.

It was in that room that I told him what had happened to me, one night when we were stretched out next to each other in the pitch black. He was very quiet and asked some questions. Then he said, 'I can't imagine someone ever wanting to hurt you like that,' and I believed him. It can't have been easy for him to hear, I've heard enough disclosures from loved ones to understand that. But he took care of me through that moment and made me feel safe.

Our life together is not perfect. I still have nightmares, odd trauma symptoms. My memory and concentration are a lot worse than they were before the rape, which can make me a truly exasperating partner. And that's before even getting to the normal challenges of being a couple, a same-gender couple, an interracial pairing and the fact we have different opinions on which way the toilet paper goes. But it's also far more fun than I'd ever imagined I'd have with a partner after being raped, and the taking care of each other is worth it.

Epilogue

When your rape is reported immediately, as mine was, the medical examination is only not about your health. It is also about evidence. Your body is the scene of a crime, and the police will want it swabbed, prodded and documented before the evidence is destroyed.

This usually happens at a SARC, or Sexual Violence Referral Unit, one of many centres dotted around the UK. In my case, even though I lived in the city, I was taken out past the fields and farms in a police car. Halfway through the ride the police officer driving me made a rape joke in a misguided attempt to break the ice, and I found myself laughing automatically. We arrived at a set of buildings in the countryside. They looked as though someone had tried to build a 1960s brutalist building on a 1980s public services budget. In other words, grim.

The door was opened by two extremely kind and extremely tired women. It can't have been later than six in the morning. What followed was upsetting and procedural. I couldn't let them swab me completely. I was injured but was so numb that I didn't discover it until I went home, so couldn't tell them. They gave me tea with milk in it (I'm lactose intolerant) and a chicken Pot Noodle. I wanted to ask what happened to vegan rape victims. Presumably they take what they are given.

After a head-spinning amount of prodding, shuddering and admin (there is so much admin in being the victim of a serious crime), the police officer asked if I wanted to be dropped home. I checked my phone and asked her to drop me off at my university. With luck I would make my 9.30am lecture.

'Are you sure that's what you want?' she asked. I nodded firmly. I wanted my life back to normal.

The hospital had prescribed me a whole suite of medications to prevent me contracting HIV, which I shoved to the bottom of my bag in case anyone noticed them. I had to take two tablets in the morning and one in the afternoon, as well as anti-nausea and anti-diarrhoea capsules to deal with the side effects. The sexual health clinic would do a blood test to make sure my liver was dealing well with all these chemicals, and schedule follow up tests in three months for HIV, syphilis, gonorrhoea and chlamydia.

It was the longest three months of my life. As a bisexual man, the spectre of HIV stigma has never been far from my life. I've had people ask if I were positive before they even asked my name. I've had men physically attack me because I was one of the men who 'give innocent women AIDS'. And as a Zimbabwean I don't even know how many members of my family have died of AIDS-related illnesses. My father still calls it 'the Disease,' and deaths surrounding it are shrouded in euphemism and mystery.

Intellectually I knew that, living in the UK, it would not be a death sentence to be HIV positive. But the feeling of having been infected through rape felt like a further invasion. I wanted to scrub the rapist out of every part of my body, and the idea that he might have altered my body forever made me want to scream.

HIV takes a while to be detectable on a test. I had to be patient.

On the day of the test, I walked to the sexual health clinic. The rooms were narrow and sometimes windowless, and I went in petrified that I was going to be dismissed again, that my care would be doled out grudgingly and sardonically. That this time, there wouldn't even be a Pot Noodle.

Instead, I met Justine. I wish I remembered more about Justine. I know she was blonde and tallish and that her room in the clinic was low ceilinged, so that it felt like a sterile cave with the light sliding in sideways. But mostly I remember her eyes; very large and very honest. I remember the way she wasn't afraid to look at me.

On the day I went in for my last blood test she asked all the questions on her form, then set her papers down.

'Do you have anything you need to ask me?' she said.

'Am I going to be okay?'

The question slipped out before I could stop it. I cringed. Of course she couldn't tell that. The tests weren't back. There were lots of things that could still go wrong. And how stupid, how pathetic, how much like a *patient* I sounded. But it was an honest question. It's a question I suspect everyone who experiences sexual violence will ask at some point.

Justine put her hand on my arm. It was the first time a medical professional had touched me other than to take blood, do a swab, or perform an examination. It was the first time a doctor had touched me as a person, rather than a patient or a crime scene. I looked up into her face.

'Yes,' she said. 'Yes, you absolutely are going to be okay.'

I don't remember exactly what happened next. That means I cried, and I'm too ashamed to remember it. But I do remember leaving the clinic, noticing the sun had come out and was shining off freshly painted hospital buildings, and feeling the beginnings of something like hope.

Am I going to be okay?

There are so many questions still surrounding how we love male survivors. So many discussions are waiting to be had about what we need from the people around us, and what we have to give to our communities and loved ones. Justine's answer to me was right, and I used to describe myself as lucky. Many male survivors have a far harder time of it than I have.

But I wasn't lucky. I was well supported, and that did not happen by accident. It happened because of the friends who took care of me in those first months after the rape. Because of the tutors, teachers and lovers who cared just as much about my dignity as my wellbeing. Because of colleagues who have graciously allowed my experience to sit alongside theirs and brought curiosity to the conversations we have together.

I am not healed, not completely, perhaps not ever. I still have so many questions which may never be answered completely. But I am also not alone in asking them.

If we can offer this to each other; if we can face the male survivors in our lives with compassion, curiosity and courage, we can answer that first question at least, just as Justine answered it for me.

Yes. We are going to be okay.

References

Introduction

1. "Statistics about sexual violence and abuse" *Rape Crisis*. rape-crisis.org.uk/get-informed/statistics-sexual-violence/. Accessed 29 July 2022.
2. "The 1 in 6 Statistic" *1in6*. 1in6.uk/unwanted-sexual-experiences/the-1-in-6-statistic/ Accessed 14 June 2022.
3. "Sexual Assault and the LGBTQ Community" *Human Rights Campaign*. hrc.org/resources/sexual-assault-and-the-lgbt-community. Accessed 14 June 2022.
4. Lisak, D., & Miller, P. M. (2002). Repeat rape and multiple offending among undetected rapists. Violence and Victims, 17(1), 73–84.
5. Widom, C.S. & Morris, S. (1997). Accuracy of adult recollections of childhood victimization part 2. Childhood sexual abuse. Psychological Assessment, 9, 34-46.
6. "Half of Men Have Had Unwanted Sexual Experiences, UK Study Finds" Kevin Rawlinson, *The Guardian*, 16 February 2021. theguardian.com/society/2021/feb/16/half-men-unwanted-sexual-experiences-uk-study-mankind. Accessed 14 June 2022.

Chapter 1

1. McGuffey, C. S. (2005). Engendering Trauma: Race, Class, and Gender Reaffirmation after Child Sexual Abuse. Gender & Society, 19(5), 621–643.
2. Ibid.
3. Strega, Susan et al, "Connecting father absence and mother blame in child welfare policies and practice." Children and Youth Services Review, July 2008.
4. McGuffey, Engendering Trauma, p 632.
5. "Sexual Offences Victim Characteristics, England and Wales – Office for National Statistics" Nick Stripe, Office for National Statistics, 18 March 2021. ons.gov.uk/peoplepopulationandcommunity/crimeandjustice/articles/sexualoffencesvictimcharacteristicsenglandandwales/march2020. Accessed 14 June 2022.
6. Ibid.
7. "Statutory rape laws in Sri Lanka: the underpinning issues" Imesha Madhubhani, *Sunday Observer*, 10 September 2017. sundayobserver.lk/2017/09/10/issues/statutory-rape-laws-sri-lanka-underpinning-issues. Accessed 14 June 2022.
8. "Legacies and Lessons: Sexual Violence against Men and Boys in Sri Lanka and Bosnia & Herzegovina." *All Survivors Project*. allsurvivorsproject.org/legacies-and-lessons-sexual-violence-against-men-and-boys-in-sri-lanka-and-bosnia-herzegovina/. Accessed 14 June 2022.
9. "British Women Are Travelling to The Gambia for Relationships with Black Men — I Have Learnt to Not Judge Them" *inews*, Seyi Rhodes, 28 September 2020. inews.co.uk/culture/television/sex-on-the-beach-channel-4-documentary-gambia-holiday-british-women-tourism-seyi-rhodes-664083. Accessed 14 June 2022.

Chapter 2

1. Wakelin, Anna & Long, Karen. (2003). Effects of Victim Gender and Sexuality on Attributions of Blame to Rape Victims. Sex Roles. 49. pp. 477-487.

2. Jacques-Tiura, Angela J., Antonia Abbey, Rhiana Wegner, Jennifer Pierce, Sheri E. Pegram, and others. 2015. "Friends Matter: Protective and Harmful Aspects of Male Friendships Associated with Past-Year Sexual Aggression in a Community Sample of Young Men," American Journal of Public Health, 105.5: 1001–7. doi.org/10.2105/AJPH.2014.302472.

3. Banyard, V. L.; Moynihan, M. M.; Walsh, W. A.; Cohn, E. S.; Ward, S. (2010). Friends of Survivors: The Community Impact of Unwanted Sexual Experiences. Journal of Interpersonal Violence, 25(2) p. 252.

4. Robinson, S., Anderson, E. & White, A. The Bromance: Undergraduate Male Friendships and the Expansion of Contemporary Homosocial Boundaries. Sex Roles 78, 94–106 (2018).

5. Ibid.

6. "The Nature of Violent Crime in England and Wales" *Office for National Statistics*, 2020. ons.gov.uk/peoplepopulation-andcommunity/crimeandjustice/articles/thenatureofviolent-crimeinenglandandwales/yearendingmarch2020. Accessed 3 August 2022.

7. Abelson, Miriam J. 2014. "Dangerous Privilege: Trans Men, Masculinities, and Changing Perceptions of Safety," Sociological Forum (Randolph, N.J.), 29.3: 549–70. doi.org/10.1111/socf.12103. p. 558

8. Ibid. p. 561

9. Proeve, Michael (2009). A Preliminary Examination of Specific Risk Assessment for Sexual Offenders Against Children. Journal of Child Sexual Abuse, 18(6), 583–593. doi:10.1080/10926770903307898

10. Jenny Cann; Caroline Friendship; Lynsey Gozna (2007). Assessing crossover in a sample of sexual offenders with multiple victims., Journal of Criminal Psychology, 12(1), 149–163. doi:10.1348/135532506x112439

11. Keith Soothill, Brian Francis, Barry Sanderson, Elizabeth Ackerley, Sex Offenders: Specialists, Generalists—or Both?, The British Journal of Criminology, Volume 40, Issue 1, January 2000, pp. 56–67.

12. Madeleine Black, *Unbroken*. John Blake, 2017.

Chapter 3

1. Rhys Price-Robertson, "Child Sexual Abuse, Masculinity And Fatherhood", Journal Of Family Studies, 18.2-3 (2012), 130-142. doi.org/10.5172/jfs.2012.18.2-3.130. p. 135.

2. Ines Yagi and others, "Characteristics and Impacts Of Conflict-Related Sexual Violence Against Men In The DRC: A Phenomenological Research Design", Social Sciences, 11.2 (2022), 34. doi.org/10.3390/socsci11020034. p. 5.

3. Wark J, Vis JA. "Effects of Child Sexual Abuse on the Parenting of Male Survivors. Trauma Violence Abuse." 2018 Dec; 19(5):499-511. doi: 10.1177/1524838016673600.

4. Armsworth, M.W. and Stronck, K. (1999), "Intergenerational Effects of Incest on Parenting: Skills, Abilities, and Attitudes. Journal of Counseling & Development," 77: 303-314. doi. org/10.1002/j.1556-6676.1999.tb02453.x

5. "Breaking the Silence of Conflict-Related Sexual Violence against Men and Boys: The Case of the Democratic Republic of Congo" Emma Birikorang & Fiifi Edu-Afful, *KAIPTC*, November 2019. kaiptc.org/wp-content/uploads/2020/10/20200901-faar-Final-Occasional-Paper-43_Sexual-Violence-against-Men-and-Boys.pdf. Accessed 24 August 2022.

6. "Characteristics and Impacts of Conflict-Related Sexual Violence against Men in the DRC: A Phenomenological Research Design," p.5

7. Ibid., p8.
8. Walker, Connie, "Episode 1: The Police Officer and the Priest," Stolen: Surviving St Michael's, Season 1, Spotify, spotify.com/show/7D4inq4DY144KIZN99Od6t?. Accessed 12 August 2022.
9. Ibid.
10. Ibid.
11. Janke-Stedronsky, Shonda R et al. "Association of parental status and diagnosis of posttraumatic stress disorder among veterans of Operations Iraqi and Enduring Freedom." Psychological trauma: theory, research, practice and policy vol. 8,1 (2016): 72-9.
12. Rhys Price-Robertson, "Child Sexual Abuse, Masculinity And Fatherhood", Journal Of Family Studies, 18.2-3 (2012), 130-142. doi.org/10.5172/jfs.2012.18.2-3.130. p. 135.
13. Wark J, Vis JA. "Effects of Child Sexual Abuse on the Parenting of Male Survivors. Trauma Violence Abuse." 2018 Dec; 19(5):499-511. doi: 10.1177/1524838016673600.

Chapter 4

1. Jacob, C. M. A., & Veach, P. M. (2005). Intrapersonal and Familial Effects of Child Sexual Abuse on Female Partners of Male Survivors. Journal of Counseling Psychology, 52(3), 284–297.
2. Ibid.
3. "Healing the Trauma of Male Rape Survivors and their Wives" Carl Collison, New Frame, 16 September 2019. newframe.com/healing-the-trauma-of-raped-men-and-their-wives/. Accessed 3 August 2022.
4. "Male Survivors of Sexual Violence in Kampala Demand for Better Services" Refugee Law Project. refugeelawproject.org/files/others/Male_Survivors_of_Sexual_Violence_in_Kampala_Demand_for_Better_Services.pdf. Accessed 24 August 2022.

5. "Position statement on male victims of crimes considered in the cross-Government strategy on ending Violence Against Women and Girls (VAWG)" *HM Government*, March 2019. assets.publishing.service.gov.uk/government/uploads/system/uploads/attachment_data/file/783996/Male_Victims_Position_Paper_Web_Accessible.pdf. Accessed 24 August 2022.

6. Ibid.

7. Russ Irving Fink "A Profeminist Perspective" in Michael Scarce ed., Male on Male Rape: The Hidden Toll of Stigma and Shame, New York: Insight Books, 1997, p. 222.

8. "When to suspect child maltreatment" *National Collaboration Centre for Women's and Children's Health*, July 2009. www.nice.org.uk/guidance/cg89/evidence/full-guideline-pdf-243694625. p.100.

9. "Silenced Survivors: Understanding Gay And Bisexual Men's Experience With Sexual Violence And Support Services In The UK" Sam Thomson and Meka Beresford, *SurvivorsUK*, 2021. survivorsuk.org/wp-content/uploads/2021/07/Silenced-Survivors-A-report-by-SurvivorsUK-.pdf. Accessed 6 May 2022.

10. Peggy Orenstein, *Boys And Sex*. Souvenir, 2020. p. 1685, Kindle edition.

About the Author

Tanaka Mhishi is a writer, performer and storyteller. His works with issues surrounding masculinity and trauma have been produced on screen for BBC 3 and on stages nationwide. He is the author of *This Is How It Happens*, a play about male survivors of sexual violence and the Off West End Award nominated *Boys Don't* which he co-wrote and performed in in partnership with Papertale Productions and Half Moon Theatre. Tanaka is a trustee for SurvivorsUK, a charity supporting male and non-binary survivors of sexual violence in London and across the UK. He lives in London.